I0429996

Table of Contents

Introduction:

"Success is Rented, Not Owned" unfolds as a guiding beacon in the complex landscape of personal achievement. In its introduction, the book challenges conventional paradigms by asserting that success is not a static possession but a dynamic, evolving process. The author encourages readers to redefine success beyond mere external markers, embracing a holistic perspective that encompasses personal growth, fulfillment, and the realization of one's potential.

This metaphor invites readers to view success not as a one-time acquisition but as a living commitment demanding continuous effort. Much like a rented space requires ongoing attention; success thrives on dedication and regular investment.

An underlying theme within the book is the critical importance of continuous effort and commitment in the pursuit of success.

Rejecting the notion of overnight triumph, the author underscores the value of perseverance and lifelong learning. Through vivid anecdotes and practical insights, the book instills the idea that challenges are not impediments but stepping stones, emphasizing the need for unwavering commitment to goals and values. In essence, "Success is Rented, Not Owned" unveils a paradigm shift, urging readers to approach success with a mindset of stewardship and the understanding that sustained commitment is the key to enduring achievement.

What is "Success is Rented, Not Owned"

"Success is Rented, Not Owned" is a phrase that emphasizes the transient and dynamic nature of success. The idea behind this saying is that success is not a permanent or guaranteed state; instead, it requires continuous effort, adaptability, and ongoing commitment.

It serves as a reminder that achieving and maintaining success is an ongoing process. It underscores the importance of consistent effort, adaptability, and a sense of personal responsibility in the journey towards success.

The Lease Agreement

This metaphorical framework reshapes our understanding of success, delving into the terms that define the journey toward accomplishment. As readers embark on this transformative exploration, they are invited to reconsider success not as a fixed possession but as a temporary arrangement governed by a Lease Agreement.

- **Understanding the Terms of Success:**

Traditionally, success has been measured by external markers – wealth, status, or accomplishments. However, the book prompts a shift towards a more comprehensive definition.

Success is portrayed not merely as a singular achievement but as a multi-faceted concept encompassing personal growth, emotional intelligence, and the alignment of one's goals with intrinsic values.

The terms of success, therefore, extend beyond the tangible and delve into the intangible aspects of fulfillment and purpose. The Lease Agreement encourages individuals to introspect and clarify their aspirations, ensuring that the pursuit of success aligns with their authentic selves.

By comprehending these terms, individuals gain a profound insight into the nature of their success journey, setting the stage for a more meaningful and purpose-driven pursuit.

- **Commitment as the Lease Agreement:**

At the heart of the Lease Agreement is the concept of commitment. In the context of success, commitment becomes the binding force that defines the terms of the lease.

The book expounds on the idea that success, like a rented property, requires an ongoing commitment to thrive. Just as a lease outlines the responsibilities of a tenant, commitment delineates the responsibilities of individuals on the path to success.

Commitment involves more than a surface-level dedication; it entails a deep, unwavering resolve to persevere despite challenges. The book draws on the principle of grit, emphasizing the importance of passion and perseverance over the long term.

Through real-life examples and case studies, readers are guided to embrace challenges not as setbacks but as opportunities for growth. The Lease Agreement, therefore, instills a sense of responsibility, urging individuals to honor their commitment to personal and professional development.

• **Embracing the Idea of Temporary Ownership:**

The Lease Agreement metaphor further challenges the conventional notion of ownership. Success, the book argues, is not owned but temporarily possessed. This idea of temporary ownership prompts a paradigm shift, encouraging individuals to view success as a dynamic entity that requires continuous effort and adaptation.

In the context of the Lease Agreement, the idea of temporary ownership is liberating. It alleviates the pressure associated with achieving a predefined endpoint and instead focuses on the ongoing process of growth. Success is portrayed as a journey rather than a destination, fostering a mindset of curiosity and continuous learning.

The book advocates for the cultivation of a growth mindset, where setbacks are reframed as opportunities for refinement. Embracing the idea of temporary ownership enables individuals to approach their goals with resilience, understanding that success is not a fixed state but a fluid and evolving experience.

This mindset shift empowers individuals to navigate the challenges of their journey with a sense of agency, embracing the responsibilities outlined in the Lease Agreement.

The metaphor of the Lease Agreement emerges as a powerful framework for understanding the terms of success. By delineating the nuanced aspects of success, emphasizing the centrality of commitment, and encouraging the embrace of temporary ownership, the book guides readers toward a transformative understanding of achievement.

The Lease Agreement metaphor reframes success as a dynamic and evolving process, prompting individuals to approach their goals with intentionality and responsibility.

As readers internalize the terms of success, they are equipped to navigate the complexities of their personal and professional journeys, realizing that success is not a static possession but a fluid and enriching experience governed by a commitment to continuous growth.

The Initial Deposit

The concept of the Initial Deposit emerges as a cornerstone in the pursuit of achievement. This metaphorical framework invites readers to understand success not merely as a destination but as a journey that begins with a purposeful and strategic investment.

As we delve into the intricacies of the Initial Deposit, we uncover the layers of investing in skills and education, building a foundation for success, and recognizing the profound significance of early efforts in achieving goals.

- **Investing in Skills and Education:**

The Initial Deposit, akin to the earnest money submitted at the beginning of a lease, symbolizes the commitment individuals make towards their successful journey. A central tenet of this metaphor is the idea that success requires an initial investment in skills and education.

The book asserts that acquiring knowledge and honing skills is akin to depositing the currency of potential, laying the foundation for a prosperous future.

By investing time and effort into learning, individuals accumulate the intellectual capital necessary to navigate the complexities of their chosen path. The Initial Deposit underscores the significance of proactive engagement in one's education, advocating for continuous skill development and a commitment to staying abreast of evolving trends.

• **Building a Foundation for Success:**

The metaphor of the Initial Deposit extends beyond education to emphasize the creation of a robust foundation for success. Just as a solid foundation is essential for the structural integrity of a building, the book argues that a well-constructed framework is fundamental for sustained success. This foundation is built not only on academic knowledge but also on character development, resilience, and emotional intelligence.

The book urges readers to introspect and identify their core values and passions, asserting that aligning these with their chosen endeavors is akin to laying a sturdy foundation. It emphasizes the importance of clarity in goal-setting, ensuring that the Initial Deposit is strategically directed towards aspirations that resonate authentically with the individual.

By nurturing a foundation rooted in personal values, individuals fortify themselves against the inevitable challenges on their success journey.

• **The Significance of Early Efforts in Achieving Goals:**

Within the framework of the Initial Deposit, the book highlights the profound significance of early efforts in achieving goals. Early investments, whether in education, skills, or character development, set the tone for the entire journey. The book contends that the initial strides taken on the path to success create a momentum that propels individuals forward.

Early efforts are not merely stepping stones; they are the catalysts for building confidence, resilience, and a growth mindset. Through case studies and real-world examples, the author illustrates how seemingly small actions, when made consistently and purposefully, can lead to substantial outcomes. The book encourages readers to view the early stages of their endeavors as opportunities for experimentation, learning, and adaptation.

Moreover, the author delves into the psychology of habit formation, emphasizing the significance of cultivating positive habits early on. Whether it is in the realm of time management, communication skills, or personal discipline, the Initial Deposit metaphor encourages individuals to invest in habits that align with their long-term goals. Early efforts, when focused and deliberate, lay the groundwork for habits that contribute to sustained success over time.

The metaphor of the Initial Deposit emerges as a compelling framework, guiding individuals to approach their journey with intentionality and foresight. By investing in skills and education, building a foundation rooted in values, and recognizing the importance of early efforts, individuals commit to the long-term lease of success.

The Initial Deposit metaphor resonates with the idea that success is not an arbitrary outcome but the result of strategic and purposeful investments made early in the journey.

As readers internalize the concept of the Initial Deposit, they are empowered to embark on their success journey with a sense of purpose, laying the groundwork for a lease agreement that fosters continuous growth and accomplishment.

Monthly Payments

Monthly Payments emerge as a pivotal concept, transforming the pursuit of success into a structured and sustainable endeavor. This metaphor invites readers to consider success as a leased property that requires consistent, monthly payments in the form of effort, discipline, and the pursuit of short-term goals.

As we delve into the intricacies of Monthly Payments, we unravel the layers of the metaphor, exploring the significance of consistent effort, the art of setting and achieving short-term goals, and the instrumental role of discipline and routine in the journey toward success.

- **Consistent Effort as Monthly Payments:**

The concept of Monthly Payments revolves around the premise that success is not a one-time investment but a continuous commitment. In the same way that monthly payments secure the tenure of a leased property, consistent effort becomes the currency that sustains success over time. The book posits that success is not an overnight achievement but the cumulative result of persistent, intentional actions undertaken regularly.

Readers are urged to embrace the mindset that every day presents an opportunity to make a payment towards their success. This involves a commitment to putting in the necessary work consistently, irrespective of immediate results. The metaphor underscores the importance of resilience in the face of challenges, advocating for a steadfast approach that treats each day as an installment in the ongoing lease of success.

The principle of compound effort asserts that the compounding effect of consistent daily actions can lead to exponential growth over time. Through anecdotes and real-life examples, the book illustrates how seemingly small efforts, when compounded, yield significant outcomes. This approach fosters a sustainable rhythm, transforming the pursuit of success into a series of intentional, monthly payments.

- **Setting and Achieving Short-Term Goals:**

A crucial component of the Monthly Payments metaphor lies in the art of setting and achieving short-term goals. These goals act as milestones, shaping the trajectory of the success journey and providing a sense of accomplishment along the way.

The book posits that breaking down larger objectives into manageable, short-term goals allows individuals to make regular, tangible payments toward their aspirations.

By defining clear, achievable goals, individuals create a roadmap for their success journey. To set SMART goals—Specific, Measurable, Achievable, Relevant, and Time-bound. This framework ensures that goals are well-defined, trackable, and aligned with the overarching vision. Achieving these short-term milestones becomes a form of monthly payment, reinforcing the commitment to the lease agreement with success.

The satisfaction derived from achieving short-term goals serves as motivation for continued effort. It creates a positive feedback loop, nurturing a sense of progress and momentum.

This approach not only enhances the overall experience of the success journey but also instills a mindset of resilience, as setbacks are viewed as temporary challenges on the path to achieving the next set of goals.

- **The Role of Discipline and Routine:**

Integral to the metaphor of Monthly Payments is the concept of discipline and routine. Discipline becomes the instrument that ensures the timely and consistent allocation of effort toward success. A disciplined approach, marked by routine and structure, is essential for meeting the obligations outlined in the lease agreement.

Discipline involves cultivating habits that align with the pursuit of success. This includes adhering to a structured schedule, prioritizing tasks, and practicing time management.

The transformative power of routine, emphasizes that success is often the result of small, daily habits that compound over time. By weaving discipline into the fabric of daily life, individuals make regular payments towards the lease of success.

The author provides practical insights into the cultivation of discipline, suggesting strategies such as creating a dedicated workspace, setting specific times for focused work, and minimizing distractions.

Routine, according to the book, not only facilitates the consistent payment of effort but also streamlines the journey, making it more predictable and manageable.

The metaphor of Monthly Payments emerges as a guiding principle, transforming the pursuit of success into a structured and sustainable endeavor. Consistent effort, the setting and achievement of short-term goals, and the role of discipline and routine are revealed as integral components of the metaphor, shaping the way individuals approach their success journey.

By understanding success as a leased property with monthly payments, readers are empowered to adopt a mindset of commitment and resilience. The metaphor emphasizes that success is not a one-time acquisition but a continuous journey marked by intentional, consistent effort.

As individuals embrace the concept of Monthly Payments, they embark on a transformative path where success is not merely a destination but a dynamic and evolving experience, sustained through the rhythm of disciplined, routine-based efforts and the achievement of short-term goals.

Maintenance and Upkeep

The metaphorical construct of Maintenance and Upkeep takes center stage, portraying success as a dynamic entity that requires ongoing care and adaptability. This metaphor invites readers to consider success as a property that demands constant attention and investment for its preservation.

As we delve into the intricacies of Maintenance and Upkeep, we explore the essential elements of adapting to change, the imperative of continuous learning and skill development, and the art of nurturing relationships and networking.

- **Adapting to Change:**

The metaphor of Maintenance and Upkeep underscores the reality that success, like a rented property, is subject to the forces of change. The book contends that the ability to adapt to change is a fundamental aspect of sustaining success over the long term. It urges readers to view change not as a threat but as an inherent part of the journey, requiring a proactive and resilient approach.

Adaptability involves embracing innovation, staying attuned to industry trends, and being open to new perspectives. The book provides real-world examples of individuals and organizations that have thrived by adapting to changing circumstances.

It advocates for a mindset shift that positions change as an opportunity for growth rather than a hindrance to success.

Moreover, the metaphor emphasizes the importance of self-awareness in navigating change. Individuals are encouraged to assess their strengths and weaknesses, recognizing areas that may require adaptation.

This self-awareness becomes a tool for intentional and strategic adjustments, ensuring that the property of success is not only maintained but also enhanced through the process of change.

- **Continuous Learning and Skill Development:**

Integral to the concept of Maintenance and Upkeep is the notion that continuous learning and skill development are essential components of successful stewardship.

The book posits that just as property requires regular upkeep to retain its value, individuals must invest in their intellectual capital to ensure the sustainability of success. Continuous learning becomes the currency that maintains the property of success.

The metaphor advocates for a commitment to lifelong learning, urging readers to adopt a growth mindset. This involves actively seeking opportunities for acquiring new knowledge, honing existing skills, and exploring areas of development.

The book contends that in a rapidly evolving world, success is contingent on the ability to adapt through a dedication to continuous education.

Practical strategies for continuous learning are presented, including engaging in industry-specific courses, attending workshops, and fostering a culture of curiosity.

The metaphor encourages individuals to treat learning not as a one-time effort but as a recurring investment in the maintenance of their success property. Through this commitment, individuals enhance their capacity to navigate change, reinforcing the metaphor of Maintenance and Upkeep.

• **Nurturing Relationships and Networking:**

The metaphorical lens of Maintenance and Upkeep extends beyond individual efforts to the realm of relationships and networking. The book asserts that success is not an isolated endeavor but a collaborative one, requiring the cultivation and nurturing of meaningful connections. Like tending to the landscaping of a property, building and sustaining relationships contribute to the overall health and vitality of success.

Networking is positioned as a strategic element of success maintenance, offering opportunities for collaboration, mentorship, and shared knowledge. The book delves into the art of networking, emphasizing the importance of authenticity and reciprocity in relationship-building.

It provides practical tips for effective networking, guiding individuals on how to create and sustain connections that contribute to the ongoing upkeep of success.

The metaphor underscores the significance of a robust support system, both personally and professionally. Individuals are encouraged to invest time and energy in building relationships that go beyond transactional exchanges.

These relationships become integral components of success maintenance, offering emotional support, valuable insights, and collaborative opportunities.

The metaphor of Maintenance and Upkeep emerges as a guiding principle, reshaping the understanding of success as a dynamic and evolving entity. Adapting to change, continuous learning and skill development, and nurturing relationships and networking are revealed as essential elements of success stewardship.

The metaphor emphasizes that success is not a static possession but a property that demands intentional care. By adopting a proactive approach to change, committing to continuous learning, and fostering meaningful relationships, individuals become effective stewards of their success journey.

As the metaphor of Maintenance and Upkeep takes root, individuals are empowered to navigate the complexities of their personal and professional landscapes, ensuring that the

property of success not only endures but
flourishes over time.

Avoiding Eviction

The metaphorical concept of Avoiding Eviction takes center stage, compelling readers to understand success as a property that requires vigilant stewardship to prevent stagnation and complacency.

This metaphor challenges the notion of success as a static possession, emphasizing the need for ongoing efforts to stay relevant, adaptive, and growth-oriented.

As we explore the intricacies of Avoiding Eviction, we delve into the recognition of complacency and stagnation, strategies for staying relevant, and the transformative power of embracing a growth mindset.

- **Recognizing Complacency and Stagnation:**

Avoiding Eviction begins with the critical task of recognizing complacency and stagnation— two insidious adversaries that threaten the sustained lease of success. The book contends that complacency, often born out of previous achievements or prolonged periods of comfort, can lead to a dangerous sense of entitlement.

Stagnation, on the other hand, represents a lack of growth or progress, a condition where the property of success becomes vulnerable to eviction.

The metaphor emphasizes the importance of self-awareness in identifying signs of complacency and stagnation. Readers are encouraged to reflect on their goals, achievements, and overall satisfaction to gauge whether they are in danger of becoming stagnant.

The book presents case studies and real-world examples to illustrate the consequences of overlooking these warning signs and emphasizes that recognizing complacency is the first step toward Avoiding Eviction.

- **Strategies for Staying Relevant:**

Avoiding Eviction necessitates proactive strategies for staying relevant in an ever-changing landscape. The book introduces a toolkit of adaptive measures designed to fortify the lease of success against the encroachment of complacency.

These strategies include fostering a culture of innovation, embracing technology, seeking diverse perspectives, and continually reassessing goals.

Innovation is positioned as a cornerstone for staying relevant, challenging individuals to question conventional approaches and seek novel solutions. The book provides practical insights into fostering a culture of innovation, encouraging experimentation, and creating an environment that values creativity.

Staying ahead requires a commitment to adapting to technological advancements, an awareness of industry trends, and a willingness to embrace change.

Diversity of thought is presented as a catalyst for avoiding stagnation. The book advocates for seeking out perspectives that challenge existing paradigms, fostering an environment where differing opinions are valued.

This diversity, the metaphor contends, acts as a preventive measure against the stagnation that can lead to eviction, infusing fresh ideas and perspectives into the success journey.

Continuous reassessment of goals is another crucial strategy outlined in the book. It encourages readers to regularly evaluate their objectives, ensuring that they remain aligned with evolving values, aspirations, and the broader socio-economic landscape.

The metaphor of Avoiding Eviction suggests that a proactive and intentional approach to goal-setting is essential for preventing the complacency that can jeopardize success.

- **Embracing a Growth Mindset:**

Central to the metaphor of Avoiding Eviction is the transformative power of embracing a growth mindset. The book contends that a growth mindset is an antidote to complacency and stagnation, fostering resilience, adaptability, and a continuous desire for improvement.

Individuals are urged to shift from a fixed mindset, where abilities are seen as inherent traits, to a growth mindset which views challenges as opportunities for learning and development.

The book provides practical strategies for cultivating a growth mindset, including reframing challenges as opportunities, seeking feedback, and embracing a love for learning.

Through real-world examples, readers are guided on a journey of mindset transformation, understanding that the willingness to confront challenges head-on is a key element of Avoiding Eviction.

Moreover, the book explores the role of mentorship and learning from others as a means of instilling a growth mindset. By surrounding oneself with individuals who embody resilience and a commitment to continuous improvement, individuals can absorb and internalize the mindset necessary for Avoiding Eviction.

The metaphor of Avoiding Eviction emerges as a guiding principle, transforming the understanding of success into a dynamic and adaptive journey. Recognizing complacency and stagnation, implementing strategies for staying relevant, and embracing a growth mindset become integral components of success stewardship.

The metaphor underscores that success is not a passive possession but a property that requires intentional and proactive efforts to avoid eviction. By fostering a culture of innovation, staying relevant through diverse perspectives, reassessing goals, and embracing a growth mindset, individuals become effective stewards of their success journey.

As the metaphor of Avoiding Eviction takes root, individuals are empowered to navigate the complexities of their personal and professional landscapes, ensuring that the property of success not only endures but thrives over time.

The Upgrade Option

The concept of the "Upgrade Option" suggests that success is not a one-time achievement but a commitment to constant improvement. This perspective encourages individuals to view their skills, knowledge, and strategies as upgradable assets.

In the context of personal and professional development, adopting an upgrade mindset involves a proactive approach to acquiring new skills, staying informed about industry trends, and embracing a continuous learning mentality.

The book likely emphasizes the importance of embracing change, staying relevant, and consistently enhancing one's capabilities to navigate the ever-evolving landscape of success.

- **Exploring New Opportunities:**

The idea of exploring new opportunities is fundamental to the notion that success is a rented space. Success is not merely about achieving a set goal but about remaining open to new possibilities and avenues for growth. The book likely discusses the significance of curiosity and adaptability in seizing unforeseen opportunities.

By encouraging readers to step out of their comfort zones, the author might highlight the potential for unexpected and transformative experiences that can contribute to personal and professional success.

- **Taking Calculated Risks:**

Success often involves a degree of risk-taking, and the term "calculated risks" implies a strategic and informed approach to decision-making. The book probably underscores the importance of evaluating risks, considering potential outcomes, and making informed choices that align with one's goals.

It may discuss how successful individuals are not necessarily risk-averse but rather adept at assessing and managing risks intelligently. By presenting case studies or anecdotes, the author might illustrate how taking calculated risks can lead to breakthroughs and advancements in one's journey toward success.

- **Overcoming Fear of Failure:**

The fear of failure is a common barrier to success, and the book likely addresses the psychological aspect of this fear. Success being "rented, not owned" implies that setbacks are part of the journey, and the ability to overcome failures is crucial.

The author may delve into strategies for reframing failure as a learning opportunity, building resilience, and developing a mindset that embraces challenges.

By exploring the experiences of successful individuals who faced setbacks, the book could

offer insights into how overcoming the fear of
failure is an integral part of the success process

A Journey in Collaborative Living

At the core of the book is the idea that success is not an individual endeavor but a collective journey. Collaborative living involves the conscious choice to engage with others, recognizing that diverse perspectives, skills, and experiences contribute to a richer and more robust path to success.

The author likely argues that by fostering a collaborative mindset, individuals can tap into a collective intelligence that transcends individual capabilities, creating an environment conducive to innovation and growth.

The concept of collaborative living extends beyond professional environments, emphasizing the importance of harmonious interactions in personal relationships, communities, and societal structures.

By weaving together anecdotes, case studies, and practical strategies, the book encourages readers to embrace the idea that shared success is not only more rewarding but also sustainable in the long run.

- **Importance of Teamwork and Collaboration:**

The book delves into the intrinsic value of teamwork and collaboration, illustrating how cohesive and well-coordinated teams outperform individuals in the pursuit of common goals.

The author likely explores the dynamics of effective collaboration, highlighting the synergy that arises when individuals with diverse skills and perspectives come together to tackle challenges.

Through real-world examples, the book may showcase instances where successful individuals attribute their achievements to the collaborative efforts of a dedicated team.

Teamwork is presented as more than just a functional necessity; it becomes a strategic advantage in navigating the complexities of today's fast-paced and interconnected world. The author might discuss how fostering a collaborative culture within organizations enhances creativity, problem-solving, and overall productivity.

By dissecting the components of successful collaborations, readers are guided on how to build and nurture effective teams that contribute to the collective success of each member.

• **Building a Support System:**

An integral component of collaborative living is the emphasis on building a robust support system. The book likely explores the significance of surrounding oneself with individuals who provide encouragement, guidance, and constructive feedback.

A support system extends beyond professional networks and may include mentors, friends, family, and colleagues who collectively contribute to an individual's success.

The author may delve into strategies for cultivating a supportive environment, discussing the importance of open communication, mutual trust, and shared values within personal and professional relationships.

Through practical tips and relatable anecdotes, the book offers readers insights into identifying and fostering relationships that contribute positively to their journey.

Moreover, the book may advocate for reciprocity within a support system, emphasizing the mutual benefits that arise when individuals actively contribute to the success of others.

By exploring symbiotic relationships and interconnected networks, readers are likely inspired to view their support system as a reciprocal ecosystem where collective success is celebrated and amplified.

- **Learning from Others' Experiences:**

Learning from others' experiences is a key theme in "Success is Rented, Not Owned." The book likely underscores the importance of leveraging the wisdom and lessons gained from the experiences of others.

By examining case studies, interviews, and narratives, readers are exposed to a wealth of diverse perspectives that contribute to their growth and decision-making.

The author may highlight the power of mentorship and the transformative impact of learning from those who have navigated similar challenges. By drawing parallels between the experiences of successful individuals and the reader's journey, the book creates a bridge between collective wisdom and personal development.

Through reflective exercises and storytelling, readers are encouraged to extract actionable insights from others' triumphs and setbacks, enriching their path to success.

Handling Property Disputes

Understanding the legal landscape surrounding property disputes is crucial. The book may discuss the importance of thorough documentation, adherence to local regulations, and seeking professional advice when needed. By offering case studies or real-life examples, readers can gain practical knowledge on how to approach and navigate property disputes effectively.

Moreover, the author may stress the significance of maintaining open lines of communication during disputes, fostering a collaborative environment where all parties involved can work towards a resolution. This could include tips on effective communication, active listening, and finding common ground to achieve mutually beneficial outcomes.

- **Dealing with Setbacks and Challenges:**

A central theme in the book likely revolves around the inevitability of setbacks and challenges on the path to success. Whether in property matters or other aspects of life, obstacles are presented as opportunities for growth and learning. The author may discuss the psychological impact of setbacks and the importance of reframing challenges as stepping stones rather than stumbling blocks.

Readers might be encouraged to adopt a proactive mindset when faced with setbacks, viewing them as temporary hurdles rather than insurmountable barriers. The book could explore how successful individuals have navigated challenging situations, drawing inspiration from their resilience and ability to turn setbacks into catalysts for positive change.

- **Developing Resilience and Perseverance:**

Resilience and perseverance are likely highlighted as essential qualities for individuals seeking success, especially when facing property disputes. The book might delve into the psychological aspects of resilience, providing readers with tools and strategies to build mental fortitude.

Through practical advice, the author may guide readers on developing coping mechanisms, cultivating a growth mindset, and embracing challenges as opportunities for personal and professional development.

Real-world examples of individuals who have demonstrated resilience in the face of adversity could serve as inspiration, illustrating that setbacks are not indicative of failure but rather stepping stones to success.

Perseverance, often a key factor in achieving long-term success, may be emphasized as the commitment to endure difficulties and stay focused on overarching goals.

The book could offer insights into maintaining motivation during challenging times, setting realistic expectations, and adapting strategies in response to evolving circumstances.

- **Strategies for Overcoming Obstacles:**

The book likely provides a toolbox of strategies for overcoming obstacles, not only in the context of property disputes but also in various aspects of life. These strategies may include:

1. **Problem-Solving Techniques:** Readers might learn systematic approaches to analyze problems, identify potential solutions, and implement effective strategies for resolution.

2. **Adaptability and Flexibility:** The ability to adapt to changing circumstances and be flexible in one's approach is crucial. The book may explore how successful individuals have embraced change and adjusted their strategies when facing unexpected challenges.

3. **Collaboration and Networking:** Collaborative efforts and building a network of support are likely discussed as powerful tools for overcoming obstacles. This could involve seeking advice from mentors, connecting with industry professionals, and leveraging collective intelligence.

4. **Learning from Failure:** Failure is portrayed as a valuable teacher. The book might encourage readers to view failures not as endpoints but as opportunities to learn, adapt, and improve.

5. **Goal Setting and Planning:** Setting clear goals and creating actionable plans can help individuals navigate challenges more effectively. The book may offer practical guidance on goal setting, prioritization, and time management.

The book is likely to provide a comprehensive guide on handling property disputes, dealing with setbacks, developing resilience, and employing strategies for overcoming obstacles.

By intertwining practical advice, real-life examples, and a holistic approach to success, the author aims to empower readers with the tools and mindset needed to navigate challenges and achieve sustainable success in various aspects of their lives.

Personalizing the Space

The concept of personalizing the space of success goes beyond conventional definitions of achievement. The book likely encourages readers to consider success as a deeply personal and subjective experience, one that is intimately tied to individual aspirations, values, and purpose.

Readers may find guidance on identifying and understanding their core values, beliefs, and passions. The author may suggest reflective exercises to help individuals gain clarity on what success means to them personally.

By creating a personalized roadmap, readers can navigate the complexities of their unique journey, embracing the idea that success is not a one-size-fits-all concept but a canvas waiting to be painted with individual strokes.

- **Aligning Success with Personal Values:**

One of the central themes likely explored in the book is the alignment of success with personal values. Success, in this context, is presented as more than just a collection of achievements; it's a reflection of one's authenticity and commitment to principles that matter deeply.

The author may delve into the process of identifying and prioritizing personal values. This involves understanding what truly matters, both personally and professionally. Through real-life examples and practical exercises, readers might be guided to make intentional choices that resonate with their values, ensuring that each step toward success is aligned with a sense of purpose and authenticity.

By aligning success with personal values, individuals are encouraged to cultivate a more meaningful and sustainable journey. This theme likely addresses the potential pitfalls of pursuing success without considering its alignment with one's core beliefs, illustrating how true fulfillment emerges when achievements are in harmony with one's authentic self.

- **Finding Fulfillment in Achievements:**

While external markers of success can be significant, the book probably emphasizes the importance of finding fulfillment within the journey and the accomplishments themselves. Readers might be guided to shift their focus from external validation to internal satisfaction, recognizing that genuine fulfillment arises when achievements are personally meaningful.

The author may explore the psychology of fulfillment, discussing how the pursuit of purpose-driven goals contributes to a sense of accomplishment and joy. Practical strategies for celebrating achievements, both big and small, may be provided, fostering a mindset that appreciates the journey as much as the destination.

The book could also address the potential challenges of tying self-worth solely to external achievements, encouraging readers to seek fulfillment within the process of growth and self-discovery.

- **Balancing Work and Personal Life:**

In the intricate dance of success, the book likely delves into the crucial aspect of balancing work and personal life. The author may acknowledge that success is not solely defined by professional accomplishments but is an integration of various facets, including personal relationships, well-being, and leisure.

The book could provide practical advice on time management, setting boundaries, and prioritizing activities that contribute to both personal and professional growth. Through anecdotes and case studies, readers may gain insights into how successful individuals have navigated the delicate equilibrium between career ambitions and personal well-being.

Furthermore, the author might explore the concept of work-life integration, encouraging readers to view their personal and professional lives as complementary rather than conflicting. The book may present strategies for avoiding burnout, fostering resilience, and nurturing supportive relationships that contribute positively to overall success.

- **Incorporating Personal Narratives:**

To drive these themes home, the book might incorporate personal narratives and interviews with individuals who have successfully personalized their journeys to align with their values. By sharing diverse stories, the author aims to inspire readers to embrace their uniqueness and approach success with a sense of individuality.

These personal narratives could encompass a range of experiences, from individuals who have found fulfillment in unconventional career paths to those who have successfully navigated the challenges of work-life balance.

By weaving these stories into the broader narrative, the book creates a tapestry of inspiration and practical insights that readers can draw upon in their pursuit of personalized and fulfilling success.

The book likely offers a rich exploration of personalizing the space of success, emphasizing the importance of aligning success with personal values, finding fulfillment in achievements, and balancing work and personal life.

Through a blend of reflective exercises, practical strategies, and real-life stories, the author invites readers to view success as a canvas awaiting their unique touch.

By embracing personalization, individuals can navigate their journey with authenticity, purpose, and a deep sense of fulfillment, understanding that success, in its truest form, is not a fixed destination but a dynamic and personalized adventure.

The Neighborhood Effect

The Neighborhood Effect is a central theme in the book, suggesting that success is not an isolated achievement but a product of the environment in which individuals immerse themselves. The author likely explores how the people, culture, and values of one's surroundings shape and influence the trajectory of success. By understanding and actively participating in the Neighborhood Effect, readers are guided to harness the power of their environment as a catalyst for personal and professional growth.

• **Surrounding oneself with Positive Influences:**

The book probably advocates for the intentional cultivation of a supportive and positive network. Surrounding oneself with positive influences becomes a crucial aspect of navigating the Neighborhood Effect. The author may discuss the significance of curating a circle of individuals who inspire, motivate, and uplift. This could include mentors, colleagues, friends, and family members who contribute positively to one's mindset and aspirations.

Readers might find practical advice on how to identify and foster relationships with positive influences. The book could explore the characteristics of individuals who radiate positivity, resilience, and a growth mindset.

By weaving in anecdotes and case studies, the author creates a compelling narrative that emphasizes the transformative power of surrounding oneself with those who share a similar commitment to success.

- **Cultivating a Success-Oriented Environment:**

Cultivating a success-oriented environment is presented as a proactive and intentional endeavor in the book. The author likely discusses how the physical and mental spaces we inhabit play a pivotal role in shaping our mindset and influencing our actions. Whether it's the workspace, home environment, or digital spaces, the book may provide insights into creating an atmosphere that fosters productivity, creativity, and a sense of purpose.

Practical strategies for designing a success-oriented environment could include organizing workspaces, setting goals, and incorporating elements that inspire and energize. The book may delve into the psychological impact of the surroundings, exploring how a well-crafted environment can positively influence focus, motivation, and overall well-being. Through actionable tips, readers can learn to tailor their surroundings to align with their goals and aspirations.

- **The Impact of Relationships on Success:**

Relationships, both personal and professional, are likely dissected in the book as key contributors to the Neighborhood Effect. The author may explore how various relationships, from mentors and collaborators to friends and family, shape the trajectory of success. The book could delve into the idea that success is not only an individual pursuit but a collective endeavor enriched by meaningful connections.

Through case studies and personal narratives, readers may gain insights into how successful individuals have leveraged their relationships for mutual growth. The author might emphasize the reciprocal nature of impactful connections, illustrating how the exchange of ideas, support, and encouragement within a network contributes to the overall success of its members.

Furthermore, the book may address the potential challenges and pitfalls in relationships, guiding in navigating conflicts, setting healthy boundaries, and fostering authentic connections. By understanding the dynamics of relationships within the Neighborhood Effect, readers can make informed choices about the individuals they choose to surround themselves with on their journey to success.

- **Creating a Virtuous Cycle:**

The Neighborhood Effect, as presented in the book, likely operates as a virtuous cycle. Positive influences, a success-oriented environment, and impactful relationships synergistically contribute to ongoing personal and professional development. The author may explore how individuals can actively contribute to this cycle by being intentional in their choices, fostering a sense of community, and giving back to their network.

The book might discuss the reciprocity inherent in the Neighborhood Effect, where individuals who benefit from positive influences and supportive relationships are encouraged to pay it forward. Through examples of successful individuals who have actively contributed to their communities, readers may be inspired to become active participants in creating a positive and thriving neighborhood for success.

• **Navigating Challenges within the Neighborhood Effect:**

While the book extols the virtues of positive influences and success-oriented environments, it likely acknowledges the inevitability of challenges and conflicts within the neighborhood.

The author may provide strategies for navigating such challenges, emphasizing the importance of resilience, effective communication, and conflict-resolution skills. By addressing potential pitfalls, the book equips readers with the tools needed to maintain a healthy and constructive neighborhood for success.

The book offers a compelling exploration of the Neighborhood Effect, emphasizing the profound impact of one's environment and relationships on the journey to success. The book provides readers with actionable insights on surrounding oneself with positive influences, cultivating a success-oriented environment, and recognizing the transformative power of relationships.

By understanding and actively participating in the Neighborhood Effect, individuals can navigate their path to success with intentionality, authenticity, and a deep appreciation for the collective nature of achievement.

Through a blend of theory, practical advice, and real-life examples, the author invites readers to reimagine success as a dynamic interplay between personal aspirations and the powerful influences of the neighborhood.

The End of the Lease

A stage in the dynamic process of success where transitions and changes are inevitable. This pivotal theme emphasizes the transient nature of success, encouraging readers to embrace preparation, reflection, and strategic planning for the next phase of their journey.

The metaphorical notion that success is rented, not owned, sets the stage for an insightful exploration of how individuals can effectively navigate The End of the Lease.

- **Preparing for Transitions and Changes:**

The End of the Lease signifies a period of transition and change, and the book likely guides readers through the importance of preparing for these inevitable shifts in their journey toward success.

The author may highlight the significance of cultivating adaptability, resilience, and a forward-thinking mindset.

Preparing for transitions involves a multi-faceted approach. The book could provide practical advice on staying informed about industry trends, anticipating potential challenges, and honing skills that will be valuable in the evolving landscape.

Through case studies and real-world examples, readers may learn how successful individuals have navigated periods of transition, drawing inspiration from their ability to embrace change and proactively prepare for new opportunities.

The author may also delve into the emotional and psychological aspects of transitions, offering strategies for managing uncertainty and maintaining a positive outlook during times of change. By fostering a proactive and adaptive mindset, individuals can approach the end of the lease as an opportunity for growth rather than a period of uncertainty.

• **Evaluating the Journey and Accomplishments:**

The end of a lease prompts a natural inclination for reflection. The book likely encourages readers to evaluate their journey and accomplishments, fostering a sense of gratitude for the successes achieved and lessons learned along the way.

The author may guide readers through a comprehensive self-assessment, helping them recognize the skills developed, challenges overcome, and personal growth experienced during the lease period.

Reflection may extend beyond individual accomplishments to encompass the broader context of success. The book could discuss the impact of collaborative efforts, acknowledging the contributions of mentors, colleagues, and support networks.

By engaging in a thoughtful evaluation of the journey, readers can gain insights into their strengths, weaknesses, and areas for continued development.

Practical exercises and reflection prompts may be incorporated to facilitate this self-assessment process. The book could provide a framework for individuals to document their achievements, challenges, and the lessons gleaned, creating a valuable resource for future planning and personal development.

- **Planning for the Next Phase of Success:**

A significant portion of the book is likely dedicated to guiding readers through the strategic planning process for the next phase of success. The end of the lease is portrayed as a transition point that opens doors to new opportunities and challenges. The author may offer a structured approach to envisioning and planning for the future, incorporating both short-term and long-term goals.

Strategic planning involves setting clear objectives, identifying key priorities, and aligning them with personal and professional values. The book could explore the importance of setting realistic and measurable goals, acknowledging the potential for adjustments as circumstances evolve. Through case studies, readers may gain insights into successful individuals who effectively navigated transitions by developing and executing well-thought-out plans.

The author may delve into the creation of action plans, emphasizing the importance of breaking down overarching goals into manageable steps. Practical tips on time management, resource allocation, and collaboration may be provided to enhance readers' ability to execute their plans effectively.

Moreover, the book could explore the role of innovation and creativity in planning for the next phase of success. Encouraging readers to think beyond conventional approaches, the author may inspire a mindset that welcomes new ideas, embraces change, and adapts to emerging opportunities.

- **Embracing Flexibility and Iteration:**

While planning for the next phase of success is crucial, the book likely recognizes the importance of flexibility and iteration. Success is portrayed as a dynamic and evolving process, and the author may advocate for an adaptive mindset that allows for course corrections based on feedback and changing circumstances.

The book could explore the concept of agile planning, where individuals remain open to learning, adjust their strategies when necessary, and view challenges as opportunities for innovation. By embracing flexibility, individuals can navigate uncertainties and capitalize on unforeseen possibilities, ultimately contributing to a more resilient and sustainable approach to success.

- **Cultivating a Growth Mindset:**

Throughout the discussion of The End of the Lease, the cultivation of a growth mindset may emerge as a central theme. The book likely encourages readers to view challenges as opportunities for learning and development, fostering a mindset that thrives on continuous improvement.

The author may draw on psychological principles to underscore the impact of a growth mindset on resilience and adaptability. Through anecdotes and real-life examples, readers may gain a deeper understanding of how individuals with a growth mindset approach transition with a sense of curiosity and a commitment to self-improvement.

The book offers a comprehensive exploration of The End of the Lease, a critical phase in the dynamic process of success. The book guides readers through the preparation for transitions and changes, encourages reflective evaluation of the journey and accomplishments, and provides a strategic framework for planning the next phase of success.

By embracing adaptability, fostering a growth mindset, and recognizing the interconnected nature of success, individuals can navigate The

End of the Lease with intentionality and resilience. Through a blend of practical advice, reflective exercises, and inspiring stories, the author empowers readers to approach transitions as opportunities for growth, ensuring that the journey toward success remains dynamic, fulfilling, and personally meaningful.

Passing the Keys

This theme revolves around the cyclical nature of success and the responsibilities that come with achieving it. The metaphorical idea that success is rented, not owned, sets the stage for an insightful exploration of the significance of mentoring, giving back, legacy building, and understanding the cyclical nature of success.

- **Mentoring and Giving Back:**

The notion of passing the keys implies a transition of knowledge, experience, and opportunities to the next generation. The book likely emphasizes the transformative impact of mentoring, not only on the mentees but also on the mentors themselves.

Through mentoring, individuals who have achieved success can share their insights, lessons learned, and practical wisdom with those aspiring to follow in their footsteps.

Mentoring is portrayed as a symbiotic relationship where both parties benefit. The author may delve into the qualities of effective mentors and the responsibilities they bear in guiding and supporting their mentees. The book could explore how mentoring fosters a sense of community and shared success, contributing to the overall growth of individuals and the broader community.

Giving back, another integral aspect of passing the keys, may take various forms, including philanthropy, community engagement, or contributing to educational initiatives. The book likely explores the idea that success is not only measured by individual accomplishments but also by the positive impact one can have on others and the community at large.

Practical advice on establishing mentorship programs, creating opportunities for knowledge-sharing, and actively participating in community initiatives may be provided. By inspiring individuals to pass on their keys through mentoring and giving back, the book fosters a culture of shared success and collective growth.

- **Legacy Building and Leaving a Mark:**

Building a legacy is a key theme in "Passing the Keys." The book likely discusses the enduring impact individuals can have by intentionally shaping their actions and contributions. Legacy building goes beyond individual achievements; it involves creating a lasting imprint that influences future generations.

The author may explore how successful individuals can consciously craft their legacy by aligning their actions with their values and contributing to causes that resonate with their beliefs. Through anecdotes and case studies, readers may learn about the strategies employed by individuals who have left a lasting mark in their respective fields.

Legacy building is presented as a dynamic and intentional process, requiring individuals to reflect on their values, passions, and the mark they want to leave on the world. The book may offer practical exercises to guide readers through the process of identifying their legacy and implementing actions that contribute to its realization.

Moreover, the book may delve into the concept of leaving a mark in both professional and personal spheres. This could involve mentoring the next generation, making meaningful contributions to the community, or championing causes that align with one's values.

By highlighting the potential for positive impact beyond individual success, the author encourages readers to consider the broader implications of their actions.

- **Understanding the Cyclical Nature of Success:**

Central to the theme of Passing the Keys is the understanding that success is a cyclical and interconnected journey. The book likely explores how the keys to success, once passed, contribute to a continuous cycle of growth, learning, and achievement. This cyclical nature emphasizes the reciprocity inherent in the success journey, where those who have benefited from mentorship and guidance are motivated to pass on their keys to others.

The author may discuss how success is not an isolated event but part of a larger ecosystem where individuals contribute to each other's growth. Understanding the cyclical nature of success involves acknowledging that the keys passed on are not lost but are continually circulated, fostering a culture of shared success.

Practical insights into building and sustaining a supportive community may be provided. This could involve creating networks, participating in industry collaborations, and actively engaging in mentorship programs. Through the exploration of successful individuals who have embraced the cyclical nature of success, readers can gain inspiration on how to contribute to and benefit from this interconnected journey.

- **Embracing Humility and Continuous Learning:**

Passing the Keys also implies a sense of humility and a commitment to continuous learning. The book likely underscores the importance of staying humble, recognizing that success is not a static possession but an ongoing process.

Humility involves acknowledging that there is always more to learn and that each individual, regardless of their level of success, can benefit from the insights and experiences of others.

The author may discuss the transformative power of continuous learning, encouraging readers to seek out new knowledge, embrace diverse perspectives, and remain open to evolving trends. By fostering a culture of humility and curiosity, individuals contribute to the cyclical nature of success, creating an environment where the keys are continually passed on and shared.

Moreover, the book may address the potential challenges and pitfalls of complacency, urging readers to avoid a mindset of entitlement and instead embrace a lifelong commitment to growth and improvement.

Through practical strategies for staying humble and maintaining a hunger for knowledge, the book empowers individuals to navigate the cyclical nature of success with grace and authenticity.

Passing the Keys" offers a profound exploration of the responsibilities that come with success. By delving into the themes of mentoring, giving back, legacy building, and understanding the cyclical nature of success, the author guides readers toward a holistic and interconnected approach to their journey.

The book inspires individuals not only to achieve personal success but also to actively contribute to the success of others and leave a positive and enduring legacy. In passing the keys, individuals create a ripple effect of growth, learning, and shared success, ultimately enriching the collective experience of the success journey.

Through a blend of theory, practical advice, and inspiring narratives, the author empowers readers to view success as a dynamic and communal endeavor, emphasizing the transformative power of passing the keys to future generations.

Conclusion:

"Success is Rented, Not Owned" offers a transformative exploration of success, urging readers to reimagine their journey as a dynamic, collaborative, and lifelong commitment. By summarizing key concepts, encouraging a continuous commitment to success, and acknowledging the dynamic nature of personal and professional growth, the author creates a narrative that transcends traditional notions of achievement.

The book empowers individuals to embrace change, cultivate a growth mindset, and actively shape their success journey in alignment with their evolving values and aspirations. Through a blend of theory, practical advice, and inspiring narratives, readers are invited to embark on a journey of continuous learning, collaboration, and fulfillment, recognizing that success is not a destination but a vibrant and ever-evolving process.

www.ingramcontent.com/pod-product-compliance
Lightning Source LLC
Chambersburg PA
CBHW070807290526
45795CB00002B/655